How to Attract
Butterflies

This little book shows you how fun and easy it is to make your yard Butterfly Friendly. Learn how to get their attention with bright colored plants, sunny areas, wind protection, butterfly spas, and more...

By: Butch Spillman

TABLE OF CONTENTS

Description

From the majestic Monarch to the graceful Swallowtail, all Butterflies are beautiful. They're life cycle is very interesting too.

Remembering the butterfly, while planning your garden, will give you hours of enjoyment watching these colorful creatures flutter from flower to flower. Attracting butterflies is possible even in the most humble backyard garden.

This little book covers the butterfly's stages of life, they're habits, needs and benefits to humans. Yep, along with bee's, the butterfly pollenates plants which provide our food.

You will learn the best bright colorful flowers to plant for attracting butterflies to your garden. Learn about how they warm themselves in the sun. Learn about their need for mud puddles and protection from the wind.

This book will only take a couple of hours to read and you will be prepared to attract them, protect them, provide for them and love everything about them.

May I ask a favor? I would very much appreciate it if you would take a minute and leave an honest review of what you thought about this little butterfly book of mine. Thank you

Respectfully,
Butch Spillman, Author

INTRODUCTION
All about Butterflies

Butterflies ~ a wisp of bright color, a flutter of wings, when they pass by, they pull our heartstrings.

What could be more exquisitely beautiful than watching the elegant butterfly take to flight? The butterfly is one of God's most majestic creations and having them brings a bright note of beauty for us to enjoy.

Butterfly watching is a pastime that pleases people all around the world. There is something truly relaxing and inspiring about butterflies. If you have never taken the time to step away for a little while to sit and watch the butterflies as they flitter around, you should make it a point to do so. You won't be sorry.

From the majestic Monarch to the graceful Swallowtail, there are about 20,000 species. They are found on every continent except Antarctica. In North America alone, there are approximately 750 different varieties of the butterfly.

The Butterfly is not only a joy to look at, it is also very important to nature. However, like with so many creatures, the habitat of the Butterfly is slowly being replaced by commercial and residential development.

This is one of the reasons creating a butterfly garden is so vital. These gardens provide butterfly habitat and protection for all stages of a butterfly. From butterfly larvae to butterfly metamorphosis, it is imperative each stage of life is protected.

With this book, you will discover how creating a simple butterfly garden allows you to help protect them so they continue to provide the Earth with their stately beauty.

CHAPTER ONE
Why Do We Want to Attract Butterflies?

Butterflies are one of the most curious creatures on the planet because of their beauty and fragile resiliency. What is even more captivating than the beauty of the butterfly is our fascination with this winged insect. We certainly do not become ecstatic when seeing a fly so what is it about butterflies that draws our attention so intently?

There are millions of insects in the world and none seems to garner the attention butterflies do. Could we simply be enamored with their wide array of beautiful colors or the fanciful way they flitter through the air, seemingly without a care in the world?

No other insect has gained the honor of being the subject of countless poems, pieces of art, festivals, myths, and legends. No matter a person's age or gender, seeing a beautiful butterfly just seems to bring out a great level of admiration. There is something deep within us that wants to protect these delicate insects so we can enjoy their grandeur for as long as possible.

Perhaps, having butterflies surround us allows us a glimpse into the beauty that awaits us on the other side of this life. It reminds us that even on our worst and darkest days, there is still something beautiful to admire and think on.

If nothing else, butterflies fill our sometimes gray surroundings with splashes of color that take us back to the innocence of our childhood. For a brief moment, the world just seems better when we stop to watch a butterfly flitter on its whimsical path.

There are many interesting facts to discover when learning all about butterflies. Butterflies have been an inspiration to man as far back as time has been recorded. From folklore to religion, the butterfly has captured the interest of humans and continues to leave them spellbound.

Many people ask is a butterfly an insect and the answer to that question is yes. A simple butterfly definition states the butterfly is an insect with two large wings that are often brightly colored. The butterfly's wings remain erect when they are at rest and spread open to reveal their gorgeous design as they take to flight.

~The symbolism of the stages of a butterfly~

Not only is a butterfly a beautiful insect to look at, it is also symbolic of love, rebirth, hope, and freedom. No one can sit back and watch a butterfly's flight without feeling a sense of joy and hope build up in their heart.

Butterflies are considered a symbol of good fortune in many areas of North America, including Louisiana where people believe a white butterfly entering a home will shortly bring good luck to the occupants. Who wouldn't want a little extra luck on their side?

Butterflies have also been embraced by Christians because they allow them to easily explain the idea of a soul and how it is transformed through salvation. When the caterpillar builds its cocoon, it goes through a process that is much like death and burial. Just like Christians, the caterpillar goes through a transformation or what you could call a butterfly metamorphosis and emerges with a new identity, taking its flight to freedom.

The butterfly can also serve as a lesson for humans regarding their need for God. As the lowly caterpillar constantly searches and chews for food, so is man constantly searching and obtaining all he can in this life.

The butterfly's chrysalis represents the tomb of Jesus and once it is empty, we are reminded of His resurrection. As the butterfly finally takes to flight, he is no longer bound to chew and gnaw his way through life; he can now take flight and rise above the monetary concerns of this life just like the Christian who is transformed through salvation. We can learn a lot by observing the stages of a butterfly and how it survives in the face of insurmountable resistance.

~The resilient butterfly rises above adversity~

Because they weigh a mere 500 milligrams or so, even a drop of rain can wreak havoc on their bodies. Although they seem frail and at the mercy of nature and man, they are more resilient than most people realize. Butterflies have been known to survive bird attacks and have even risen in flight after having a wing ripped from their body. For their strength in the face of weakness, they have become a symbol of inspiration to us all.

Many people see the butterfly as a symbol of endurance. One would only need to look at the flight of the Monarch to realize what great perseverance these insects have. Each year, for thousands of years, Monarchs have taken to the skies flying some 2,000 miles from Canada to Mexico. Imagine what this insect goes through on that flight alone. How can they possibly overcome all of the obstacles they are faced with along the way?

The butterfly also stands as a symbol of our frailty as

humans, both in the physical sense and spiritual. The lifespan of the butterfly is a short one compared to some insects which reminds us to enjoy the sun and the joys of life during our brief time on Earth.

Although butterflies are the epitome of perfection and beauty, they sometimes become ravaged by life's circumstances just as we do. Sometimes, these beautiful creatures are born without one of their wings. Even in this state, they are still one of the most serene pictures of beauty this world has to offer. This is why one North American charity for disabled children uses an image of a butterfly with a torn wing as its logo.

~Butterflies inspire us to greater things~

Putting aside the symbolism and folklore, butterflies are simply inviting creatures to be around. These winged insects seem to help us better understand life and its spiritual side as we stop long enough to enjoy their fanciful flight or observe them fluttering their wings as they drink the sweet nectar from a flower.

Out of all the insects in the world, the butterfly is surely a favorite. This is why we must do all we can to help this magnificent creature survive and even thrive.

If we want to continue to enjoy the inspiration the butterfly brings to our lives, we must find ways to protect them. If each person does their part to offer a butterfly garden of safety to our winged friends, we can protect their numbers and keep them with us so their beauty will never fade.

Having butterflies around us offers us many benefits that sometimes cannot even be put into words. Before we delve further into attracting beautiful butterflies, it is helpful if we discover more about the butterfly cycle and how it provides us with the information we need so we can provide a safe haven to these amazing insects that are truly a gift from God.

CHAPTER TWO
Butterfly Facts –Why Do They Matter?

When we think about butterflies, our minds are immediately focused on sunshine, flowers, and the warmth of summer. These feelings butterflies evoke in us are one of the reasons people are so excited when they have the opportunity to see one.

Butterflies serve as a warning to us when negative environmental changes begin to occur. When the forests begin to be cut down and pollution grows in large numbers, the butterfly seems to be the creature that suffers the most. This is why this insect serves as an environmental signal of what is going wrong in the Earth.

According to the National Wildlife Federation, butterfly numbers are going down. In the last two decades alone, the beautiful Monarch butterfly has decreased in numbers by up to 90%. Individuals can get involved in helping this special creature grow in numbers simply by planting the right plants to attract these winged insects.

The endangerment and extinction of these insects is a direct result of butterfly habitat destruction, pesticide misuse, and genetic modifications to plants. The loss of these insects is much more than a simple loss of beauty in our world. Butterflies are an integral part of the environment and their loss would be a great detriment to society and the world as we know it.

~Butterfly facts that may surprise you~

Getting to know more about butterflies will help you to understand their unique and important role on Earth. The more we learn about butterflies, the more they fascinate us. Reading the following butterfly facts will help you understand even more how important it is for us to protect butterfly life as much as we possibly can.

- Many species of butterflies can taste with their feet. When they land on a plant, their feet help them know whether or not the plant will be a good food source for their young. If they like what their feet taste, they will lay their eggs there.
- A butterfly's eyes are made up of over 6,000 lenses and they are able to see some colors, such as red, violet, blue, and green. This is why they are attracted to colorful flowers.
- Butterflies have been found living on every single continent except Antarctica. They cannot survive cold climates because they cannot fly when their muscle temperature drops below 55.
- Believe it or not, a butterfly's wings are actually clear. We see their brilliant colors because of the reflection of light from the tiny scales that cover their wing surface.
- Butterflies do not eat like you and I. They have a long tongue that looks like a tube, called a proboscis. This tongue allows them to absorb their food into their bodies rather than suck it up like we might think.
- Male butterflies drink from mud puddles because this allows them to extract minerals they cannot get from the nectar of flowers. This strange behavior is called "Puddling" and a group of

males drinking from mud puddles is called a "Puddle Club."

- Butterflies are cold-blooded insects so they cannot regulate their own body temperature. This means they must be in a warm environment to be able to fly.
- Wondering how the butterfly got its name? Older writings suggest people first called a certain insect butter-colored because it was golden. Eventually, people began to include the winged insect under this same title. It is also said butterflies would often flutter around farmers when they were churning butter.

It is truly amazing to realize the transformation caterpillars go through as they change from an insignificant creature to one of great grandeur and beauty. This metamorphosis reminds us that we too can emerge from our present circumstances and rise above them.

~Butterflies benefit us more than we realize~

Everyone knows butterflies are a great stress-reducer. Just sitting watching them fly around and enjoying their beautiful colors can greatly reduce your blood pressure and give you an overall sense of well-being. Not only are butterflies so amazing to watch, they also provide us with important environmental benefits.

Butterflies love to drink the nectar from flowering plants and in doing so, they also help in pollination. When a butterfly sits on a flower and enjoys its delicious nectar, it also picks up pollen on its legs. Once the butterfly heads to the next flower, the pollen goes with them.

Many of the foods we eat must be pollinated by bees and butterflies before the fruits and vegetables begin to form. With bees already in lower numbers, it is more important than ever for us to do all we can to increase butterfly numbers across the world.

The butterfly life span involves four different stages of growth. At each of these stages, the butterfly provides a food source to birds, spiders, lizards, and other insects. Removing any part of the food chain can begin to cause serious repercussions among the creatures in that chain.

Butterflies also benefit plant life in the garden. When in the caterpillar stage, leaves are eaten as a food source.

Scientists have discovered the destruction of the leaves before fall's cool weather come in helps plants to survive longer. The chewing action also discourages some types of plants from propagating out of control and choking out other plants in the garden.

While the vast majority of butterflies do not consume anything other than plant life, there is one species that helps to keep garden aphids under control.

This butterfly, called, The Harvester, enjoys dining on aphid pests that destroy plants in the garden. Butterflies can help gardeners protect their plant life by getting rid of the aphids that cause catastrophic damage to tender plants that are trying to grow.

CHAPTER THREE
Understanding the Life Stages of a Butterfly, Butterfly Metamorphosis

Before we can fully understand how to begin attracting butterflies, it helps to know a little more about how they grow through the butterfly stages of life. Learning about the life cycle of a butterfly for kids helps us to better understand how truly extraordinary these insects are.

~The butterfly cycle all begins with a tiny egg~

The first stage in the life of a butterfly is like that of most insects – the egg. The butterfly begins its life as a tiny egg that can be round, oval, or cylindrical. If you have never had the opportunity to view a butterfly's eggs, you are going to be amazed when you do.

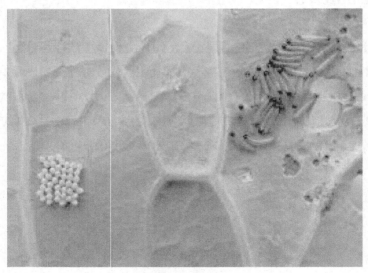

If you peer very closely at these small eggs, you will be able to see a tiny caterpillar growing inside. It is

especially easy to see a Monarch caterpillar as it grows inside the egg. Many classrooms across the country have started incorporating butterfly studies into their lesson plans because kids can see the amazing growth taking place within the butterfly egg and watch as changes keep occurring throughout the butterfly life.

Butterflies lay their eggs on leaves. As we discussed earlier in the book, they taste with their feet so they seek out plants they think will be good to eat and lay their eggs there. Once your butterfly garden is growing rapidly, you will be able to spot these eggs and enjoy watching the little caterpillar babies growing inside.

The butterfly egg is made up of a layer called the chorion. Inside the egg casing is the female butterfly's fertilized ovum. At the top of each egg, is a tiny opening called the micropyle. When you see a butterfly egg, you will be able to recognize the micropyle as a tiny depression in the top of the egg.

This opening is left behind after the male butterfly deposits its sperm. Scientists have discovered the micropyle also allows water and air to enter so the developing caterpillar is able to breathe.

Inside each egg is a yolk that provides nutrients to the growing caterpillar. The number of days it takes for a baby caterpillar to hatch depends on the species of butterfly. The average length of time spent inside the egg is about ten days.

Some species of butterflies will lay their butterfly eggs on the underside of leaves before winter arrives. The eggs remain in a somewhat dormant state through the winter and then begin to hatch with the warmth of spring. What an amazing transformation begins with the opening of each butterfly egg!

~The cute caterpillars begin to emerge~

Once the baby caterpillar has grown large enough, it will begin to eat its way out of its egg. As it munches away at the egg, it finds a way of escape so it can finally view the outside world around it.

The very first meal a baby caterpillar eats is its own egg casing. Caterpillars are in the larvae stage and they are voracious eaters. During this stage of development, all a caterpillar does is eat, eat, and eat some more.

Caterpillars are constantly chewing and eating leaves. Scientists report these larvae are able to consume around 200 times their body weight before they go to the next stage of development. This would be like the average human baby consuming about 1,400 pounds of formula in only two weeks. That is a lot of food!

The structure of a caterpillar is quite astonishing. These larvae have strong mandibles that allow them to greedily devour the foliage of plants. The caterpillar has three true legs that are used for moving and five legs that are called prolegs. The prolegs feature suction cup–like structures with hooks that allow the caterpillar to hang onto stems and leaves for easier eating.

You might think a caterpillar breathes through a nose and mouth like we humans do but that is not the case. Amazingly enough, these creatures have openings on the sides of their body that allow them to breathe. These are called spiracles and they allow for unique respiration.

When the caterpillar larva first makes its way out of the egg, it is incredibly tiny at only a few millimeters in length. Because of their unique skeletal system, a caterpillar does not grow the way we think most creatures do.

This tiny creature will shed its skin a few times during the larvae stage. The shedding of the caterpillar's skin is called ecdysis. Each new skin is called an instar and the average caterpillar will go through five instars before they reach the next stages of a butterfly.

Once the caterpillar larva has matured to its final level, it begins looking for a place to pupate. It will release all of the excrement in its digestive system before it finds a suitable location to begin the next stage of the butterfly cycle.

~The pupa stage of the butterfly starts the process of great change~

The butterfly lifespan is nothing short of miraculous to view. This is why so many people are fascinated with butterflies and want to attract them by providing favorable plant life in their garden.

The pupa stage is where the real fun begins. People of all ages cannot help but be mesmerized as they see the changes that take place during this period of the butterfly metamorphosis.

From the time the caterpillar enters the pupa stage and creates its chrysalis (Cocoon) to the time it emerges as a graceful butterfly only takes about ten to fourteen days. What a stunning transformation occurs when the mundane caterpillar transforms from its former state into one of magnificent beauty!

The word chrysalis comes from a Greek word that means gold. To make its chrysalis, the Monarch butterfly will first create a small silk pad on the bottom of a leaf or stem. This is only the beginning of what is about to be the most monumental period in the butterfly's life.

Once the silk pad has been made, the caterpillar hangs upside down and attaches itself to the silk pad, using its cremaster. It excretes a long length of silk, wrapping it around and around its cremaster (the hook like tip of a butterfly pupa, serving as an anchorage point) until the caterpillar is firmly held in place and feels secure.

Many people mistakenly believe a chrysalis is something the caterpillar creates to surround itself but this is not true. The chrysalis is the final skin that is created by the caterpillar. Once the caterpillar is securely attached to the plant, it sheds its old skin one final time and reveals the unique chrysalis that seems to enshroud it like a tomb.

When the chrysalis is first revealed, the caterpillar is in its most vulnerable state because the skin is soft. It will not be long before the chrysalis begins to harden and become the protective shell it is meant to be.

~The butterfly metamorphosis begins~

Although you cannot tell from the outside, there is a fury of activity going on inside the chrysalis. An easy way of looking at the butterfly metamorphosis is to think of recycling. If you were to pick up a plastic soda bottle and take it to your local recycling company, the plastic could be melted down and formed into something else entirely. This is much like what happens inside the chrysalis.

Without getting too scientific, the body of the caterpillar begins to break down and the cells are transformed into cells called imaginal cells. These cells are very much like our own stem cells because they can become any type of cell the butterfly needs. This process is called holometabolism and it is one of the most fascinating processes you can imagine. If only we could see inside the chrysalises to see what is happening to the caterpillar at each stage of change.

~The emergence of the most beautiful insect~

The process whereby a Monarch butterfly emerges from its chrysalis is one of the most interesting things you will ever learn about. Just before the Monarch is ready to emerge, the chrysalis becomes more transparent and you can see the beautiful colors of the wings shining through. When you see this, it is only a matter of time before the beautiful butterfly is revealed.

The chrysalis features a weak area that allows the butterfly to burst out. To begin to split open the chrysalis, the butterfly will begin to swallow air. This allows the butterfly to form a pocket of air between itself and the chrysalis shell it will leave behind.

The butterfly begins to swallow some of the air so its body becomes bigger. As the butterfly grows larger and larger, the chrysalis begins to split open and the butterfly is able to climb out.

You will be able to determine a Monarch is ready to come out of its chrysalis when you see accordion-like bands beginning to develop above the golden band near the top of the chrysalis. This means within hours, the butterfly should start to emerge and make its presence known to the world.

CHAPTER FOUR
How to Protect Butterfly Life in the Garden

Because each stage of the butterfly leads to different predators and risks, it is imperative we all understand how we can offer protection. Once you create your garden and your plant life is thriving, you are bound to discover butterfly eggs if you keep a careful check of the stems and leaves of your plants.

~How to protect those delicate butterfly eggs~

Butterfly experts understand the importance of protecting eggs. Eggs are vulnerable to insects like spiders and ants. Frogs and lizards also like to devour them. If you find a butterfly has laid eggs on one of your plants, carefully trim a small section of the plant and bring it inside.

The plant should be placed in a jar with a screen top. You can make your own using a Mason jar, an old screen, and a large rubber band. It only takes about four days before you will have several hungry baby caterpillars munching greedily on the plant you have provided them.

Protecting the butterfly eggs is an extremely important part of making sure a butterfly will be the end result. If the eggs are damaged or destroyed, this further decreases the butterfly population and it is already in low numbers.

~Protecting caterpillars in your butterfly garden~

You will never see beautiful butterflies in your garden if you do not protect the caterpillars. There are many predators who love to gobble up these poor creatures and devour them before they are able to make their transformation and take flight.

Once your garden is in place, you will eventually find caterpillars munching the leaves of the plants you have planted. To protect this vulnerable stage of life in the stages of a butterfly, it is important to cover the plants with mesh bags. These bags are fairly inexpensive and can be purchased at many home and garden retailers. Covering the plants ensures they still get water and sunshine but prevents predators from making a meal out of the caterpillars.

You will need to check your plants every couple of days to make sure they have not eaten all of the foliage and run out of food. Remember, these little guys can eat many times their weight in leaves so make sure to keep a check on them. If they run out of leaves to eat, they will die. If you find your caterpillars have eaten all of their leaves, gently remove them and place them on another plant that is full of foliage. Make sure to cover the plant.

~Protecting a butterfly chrysalis~

Once you find a chrysalis on your plants, the excitement truly begins. Sometimes, you will begin to find caterpillars in the pupa stage while others have not reached that point yet. It is vital you remove the branch the chrysalis is hanging from or the younger caterpillars could end up devouring the leaf and leaving the chrysalis catastrophically damaged.

If you choose to remove the chrysalis, make sure you remove the entire portion of the plant it is attached to. You can place it in a jar but the chrysalis needs plenty of moisture so it does not dry out. You should spray the chrysalises a couple of times a day with non-chlorinated water so they stay moist.

Seeing the butterfly emerge from its chrysalis is a magical experience you will never forget. It is special no matter how many times you have seen it happen. Once the newborn butterfly has emerged, it will be several hours before it can take flight. Its wings are wet and not fully functioning at this point. Leave it alone and watch as its wings begin to dry and harden. You will know the butterfly is ready to be released into your butterfly garden when it begins to slowly beat its wings.

Releasing butterflies into your garden is one of the most rewarding experiences you will have in butterfly gardening. As long as you have planted the right plants and flowers, the butterflies will welcome your garden as their new home and you will be able to enjoy watching them flitter about, adding splashes of beauty to your garden landscape.

CHAPTER FIVE
Butterfly Characteristics and How They Behave in a Butterfly Garden

If you have never had a butterfly garden, you may not be aware of the unique behaviors these stunning insects exhibit. Butterfly watchers know there is nothing more relaxing than sitting in a comfortable chair, watching colorful wings flutter to and fro in the garden.

There are four main behaviors butterflies exhibit while living in their butterfly habitat. Watching each of these shows just how graceful and strong these insects are. As you grow your butterfly garden, you will be able to experience all of these behaviors, along with the fanciful flight butterflies exercise as they make their way from flower to flower.

Watching butterflies is a great way to educate people of all ages. Kids and adults will enjoy watching these gorgeous creatures at all stages of life. Once your butterfly garden is in place and you have butterfly inhabitants, you will likely find yourself wanting to spend as much time outdoors as you possibly can. No one regrets spending time relaxing as they watch these colorful creatures flying around.

~Basking keeps butterflies warm~

As we have discussed, butterflies are cold-blooded insects which means their bodies do not have the ability to keep them warm. These insects must rely on the heat they absorb from the sun to be able to fly. This is why many butterflies have dark-colored bodies. This allows them to heat up hotter than the air around them.

Basking is a behavior that you will often see on sunny days in your butterfly garden. Butterflies bask when they fully stretch out their wings and relax in the sun. This is one of the most delightful behaviors because it allows us to see the beautiful designs and colors on the wingspan of the butterfly.

You will often see butterflies basking in your garden during the morning hours. Overnight, the temperatures can drop much lower, leading to the need for the butterfly to spend time absorbing the sun. If you want to see the butterflies in their most glorious position, make sure you head out to your garden early in the morning, when the sun is just starting to heat the air. The sight of them is breathtaking!

~Nectaring is an important behavior for butterflies~

A garden full of flowers will allow you to witness butterfly nectaring which is an important behavior for butterflies of all types. Nectaring occurs when the butterfly releases its tongue, called a proboscis, into the deep tube of a flower. This gives the butterfly the sweet nectar it needs for survival.

It is interesting to note, some butterflies live in areas that do not have great amounts of flower growth. Since they cannot consume the nectar from flowers, they will sip from fermenting fruit that falls on the ground.

If you find flower blooms lacking in your garden, a tray of cut up fruit will be a welcome treat to butterflies and you will be able to enjoy watching them nectaring as they sip the fruit juices and become full of nutrients. Honey water can also be given if you find yourself protecting a butterfly that has a damaged wing.

~Puddling is a behavior male butterflies exhibit~

We briefly touched upon the subject of puddling in a previous chapter but it is important to expand on this topic so you will understand what is happening if you see it.

Puddling is a behavior that involves a male butterfly drinking from a mud puddle. You might think this to be odd behavior but it is actually quite important for the survival of all butterfly species.

Puddling is not just for getting water. Many people think a butterfly is simply thirsty when drinking from a mud puddle. What the male butterfly is actually doing, is taking in vital minerals that help to ensure he is fertile. Fertile male butterflies lead to healthy fertilized eggs that become beautiful butterflies.

In your butterfly garden, you can encourage puddling when you water your plants. Make sure you create a few small mud puddles scattered throughout your garden and

your male butterflies will thank you by showing off a little puddling action now and again. This is an important behavior for the health of the male because they need the salts and minerals they absorb from these puddles.

~Understanding how do butterflies mate~

If you have ever wondered how butterflies mate, you need to read further. The mating process is almost as beautiful to discover as the butterflies themselves. A male butterfly is able to find a female by sight. When he finds her, he begins releasing his pheromones that are meant to woo her and make her attracted to him.

If you see a butterfly furiously flapping his wings faster than normal and he is around another butterfly, he is likely trying to attract her with his pheromones so he can mate with her. This is a unique moment to observe and gives great insight into the life of a butterfly and how it behaves through each stage in its life.

If the female accepts him, the male and female butterfly link with one another end to end. Once they are attached to one another, they will sometimes take flight, which is a truly beautiful sight to behold. Their flight of courtship is like a beautiful dance as they flutter along.

The two will likely remain attached to one another for a couple of hours or more. Sometimes, butterflies have been known to couple for as long as twenty-four hours. During this process, the male passes his sperm packet into the female butterfly's body.

The sperm packet is called a spermatophore and it travels down the female butterfly's egg tube, eventually making its way to each of her eggs so they are fertilized and can be laid. This love-at-first-sight courtship leads to more beautiful butterflies being released on the Earth.

Although it is romantic to think about butterfly love, the sole purpose of adult butterflies is to create the next generation of butterflies so their species does not die out.

Male butterflies are ready to mate as soon as one hour after emerging. During their life, they will mate with many female butterflies until all of their sperm is gone. Once their sperm is gone, the male butterfly will die within about six to eight weeks.

Female butterflies are ready to mate as soon as they come out of their pupa. They will only mate once in their lifetime. A female butterfly will die once all of her eggs have been laid. Should a female never mate, her life will be prolonged and she will end up dying of natural causes instead of due to laying eggs.

~The fanciful flight of butterflies~

Chances are one of the biggest reasons you want to attract butterflies is so you can see them flying around.

There is such a great sense of freedom and joy when watching these winged insects take flight.

Wondering how do butterflies fly? The answer to this question is not quite as simple as it may seem. You might think a butterfly simply flaps its wings up and down like a bird when it takes to flight but this is not the case.

Butterflies actually fly by contracting their bodies which creates a figure eight pattern with their wings. As the butterfly works to contract its body, air is forced under the wings, creating lift.

If you have ever watched a butterfly in flight, you have likely seen it take on what seems to be a truly erratic flight pattern. Sometimes, it almost looks as if the butterfly is drunk because it cannot seem to fly smoothly.

This type of flight pattern is used by the butterfly to keep it safe from bird predators. A flittering butterfly is much more difficult to catch than one that is flying in a straight pattern. Now that you know this, you will likely smile every time you see it happen.

All of these behaviors simply prove how truly clever and unique the butterfly is. Now that you know more about these delicately divine insects, it is time to begin planning your butterfly garden so you can learn how to attract these creatures and keep them around your home as much as possible. In the next few chapters, you will discover the steps you need to take so your butterfly garden will be a great attraction to butterfly life in all its stages of development.

CHAPTER SIX
How to Plan a Butterfly Garden

Planning a butterfly garden is not all that difficult, especially if you know the types of butterflies that live in your area. Each area of the country is home to different species of butterflies. To find out which ones reside in your area, you can use the online tool provided by the National Wildlife Federation. The more you understand about the butterfly life in your state, the better equipped you will be to make sure your butterfly garden offers a great food source and protection for these insects.

~Plotting the space for your butterfly garden~

One of the first decisions you will need to make in planning your butterfly garden is plotting the space. To ensure you choose the perfect space, you need to first find a location in your yard that offers as much sunshine as possible. Butterflies must have the sun or they will not be able to thrive.

Planning the size of your garden is important. You will need to decide if you simply want a small garden of flowers that attracts butterflies or if you want to provide a butterfly sanctuary so you can enjoy these insects in all stages of the butterfly cycle.

You will need to think about how much time and effort you are willing to put into your butterfly garden. If you do not have much time, a simple flower garden will likely be your best decision. If you have more time and truly want to enjoy seeing the life cycle of butterflies happen right before your eyes, then you will need to put in a little more time and effort to ensure your garden is a safe haven for all types of butterflies.

~How to diagram your butterfly garden~

Once you have found the ideal place that will be
protected from wind and will feature plenty of sunshine,
it will help if you draw up a diagram to plan out the
spacing of plants. Diagramming is especially important
if you wish for your butterfly garden to serve as a more
formal area of your yard.

Putting your ideas on paper will help you to properly
plot your garden so you will be ready to plant once you
have purchased your seeds or plants. It is always easier
to make changes on paper than to dig up plants and
move them around because you do not like their
arrangement.

Along with the garden diagram, it helps to make a list
of elements you want in your butterfly garden. A

beautiful fountain would be a welcome addition and would be a great area for you to place fruit treats, should you decide to supplement the butterflies' diet.

Your garden design can be as simple or extravagant as you like. The more thought you put into your garden now, the easier things will be when it comes time to put all the plants together.

Your butterfly garden plan should include the following elements.

- Windbreaker trees and shrubs that are planted around the garden will help to prevent wind bursts that could stop the butterflies from enjoying the garden space.
- The garden should feature a large area of flowering plants that flower in sequence so there are always brightly-colored blossoms available to provide delicious nectar to the butterflies.
- To provide protection, you should offer logs, and broad-leaved trees so the butterflies will have shelter during periods of wet weather and at night when the temperatures begin to drop lower.

Butterflies do not need a fancy garden or any expensive amenities. They are simply looking for shelter, a food source, and a place to sit and absorb the heat of the sun. Providing green plant life, flowers, trees, and logs will keep butterflies living in your garden so you can enjoy them.

Now that you know how to plan your butterfly garden, it is time to learn more about the plants that will attract butterflies to your yard. You are about to discover some of the greenery and flowers that will become beacons for butterflies of all types so your garden will be teeming with butterfly life.

CHAPTER SEVEN
Plants That Attract and Provide a Butterfly Habitat

As you begin thinking about plants for your butterfly garden, you will need to consider making sure you have both green plant life and plenty of flowering plants. If you want to create a butterfly sanctuary so you can observe the butterfly at all stages of life, you will need to provide these four elements in your garden.

- Plants for laying eggs
- Plants for caterpillar food
- Safe areas for forming chrysalises
- Flowering plants for nectar-producing

~Including butterfly host plants is important~
The first plants we will discuss are planted primarily as a host plant. The host plant provides a food and shelter source for eggs and growing caterpillars. If you want butterflies to stick around in your butterfly garden, you will need to provide an ample mix of both host and nectar plants so all stages of developing butterfly will be provided for. There are many plants you can choose from; depending on the area of the country you are planting your butterfly garden. Before choosing any

particular plant, it is important to research it and learn what growing zones it will prosper in.

~Milkweed~

Milkweed is a plant you will want to have in your garden, especially if you want to attract Monarchs. This herbaceous plant releases a milky substance, which is why it was given its name. Monarch caterpillars only eat milkweed and the females will only lay their eggs on milkweed plants so make sure you include some of these plants.

~Ornamental Grasses~

Ornamental grasses not only add depth and beauty to a butterfly garden, they also provide a place for females to lay their eggs and for baby caterpillars to munch on. There are many varieties of ornamental grass to choose from, depending on your area of the country. Consider choosing varieties such as Panicum, Schizachyrium, Muhlenbergia, or Carex. These grasses will allow females to safely lay their eggs and will provide areas for butterfly mating.

~Baptisia~

When you first see this plant with its beautiful Indigo blooms, you may think it would be planted for nectar. Although it does offer tons of beautiful flowers, butterflies are not interested in the Baptisia for this reason. This plant is a host plant and provides food and shelter for caterpillars. It will offer protection for larvae and eggs but will also add a beautiful splash of color to your butterfly garden.

~Pipe Vine~

This vine is a popular choice for gardeners because of its unique look and variegated leaves. If you have never seen a Pipe Vine plant, you will be truly amazed when you see the peculiar flowers it produces. This is a host plant that will offer unique variety to your garden and help attract the beautiful Pipevine Swallowtail.

~Herbs~

Herbs are great plants for providing hosts to caterpillars of all types. Some of the best herbs to plant include dill, parsley, fennel, caraway, cilantro, and anise. Just as herbs tantalize our taste buds with their aroma and taste, they also offer a smorgasbord of attraction for all types of caterpillars. If you also want to plant herbs for cooking, consider using a windowsill so butterflies cannot lay their eggs on your herb plants.

~Make sure flowers abound in your butterfly garden~

It is a must for you to include a wide array of colorful nectar-producing flowers in your butterfly garden. When adult butterflies are searching for nectar, they will look for the following.

- Flowers with short tubes
- Flowers in colors of red, pink, purple, blue, and yellow
- Clusters of flowers or flowers with flat tops

It is important to choose a wide array of flowering plants that will bloom in succession so there will always be beautiful blossoms available to provide sweet nectar to butterflies of all types. When you see the beauty of these flowers, you will not be able to help yourself in filling your garden with their delightful blooms. As with the host plants, make sure to carefully research your options so you can be sure the flowers you choose will grow in your planting zone.

~Butterfly Bush~

If you only plant one single plant in your butterfly garden, you need to make sure you include the Butterfly Bush. This is hands down, the number one plant you need to consider putting in your garden. This bush plant attracts many different species of butterflies, providing them with sweet nectar. This is a hardy bush that can support hundreds of butterflies feeding on it at once. The bright blooms will be a welcome attraction to your garden and you will love seeing all the butterfly life it attracts.

~Butterfly Flower~

Any time you see butterfly in the title of a plant, you know it will be a good one to include in your garden. Although it has a generic name, the Butterfly Flower is anything but. The colorful blooms provide sweet nectar to the adult butterflies and the foliage offers food for caterpillars as they grow and mature. The reason this plant offers such a great level of protection to butterflies is the white latex that is found in the stems. This substance tastes terrible to caterpillar predators so they will avoid it.

~Coneflower (Echinacea)~

This beautiful perennial can be planted in almost every area of the United States. It provides a beautiful purple bloom that entices adult butterflies to consume its sweet nectar. This flower alone will attract around thirty different species of butterflies. Since it is a perennial, you will only need to plant it once and it will keep coming back over and over.

~Aster~

Asters begin to bloom late in summer and through fall. With their beautiful purple and lilac-colored blossoms, they are a great attraction for butterflies. Not only do these gorgeous blooms offer sweet nectar to butterflies, they also provide a host for caterpillars with their rich green foliage. Be sure to include this beauty in your butterfly garden and you will soon witness all of the butterfly stages of life.

~Salvias~

Salvias offer uniquely shaped blooms in a variety of colors. If you have never seen this gorgeous plant, you will want to research it and consider including it in your butterfly garden. This plant offers a very long bloom time and is extremely tolerant of drought. Not only does this plant attract butterflies, it is also considered a tasty delight for hummingbirds. With this plant, you will attract even more beautiful creatures to your garden for butterflies.

~Lantanas~

Lantanas are perennials that bloom all summer long. They offer a beautiful color variety of sunshiny yellows and oranges. This flowering plant is sure to bring in tons of butterflies to your garden and like the Salvias, Lantanas also attract hummingbirds. Many people prefer to plant perennials because they can plant once and then watch their blooms come back year after year.

~Black-Eyed Susan~

With its curious name and bright yellow blooms, the Black-Eyed Susan is a butterfly garden favorite. It is interesting to note, this flower has patterns on its petals that only the butterfly can see. No wonder this special plant is a butterfly favorite. The reason the butterflies can see this special pattern is they are able to see with ultraviolet vision. Butterflies just might be the coolest insect on the planet!

~Goldenrod~

Goldenrod is a flowering plant that blooms in the late summer and fall. Goldenrod is a plant that many people mistakenly believe they are allergic to. This plant grows around the same time as ragweed which is typically the culprit for causing allergy attacks in those who deal with seasonal allergies. If you truly have an allergy to Goldenrod, skip this plant. This plant brings a bit of sunshine to your butterfly garden and you will find butterflies of all types are drawn to it.

~Daisy~

Daisies are a truly easy flower to grow and are often seen growing wild along the sides of roads. Daisies are one of those plants that not only provide delicious nectar, they also offer hosting for eggs and caterpillars. Although there are many varieties of Daisies, butterflies seem to prefer the Ox-Eye Daisy, also known as the Common Daisy. The petals of these daisies are white and they have a yellow center. They are a hardy plant that adds height to your butterfly garden design.

~Plant spacing for your butterfly garden~

Plant spacing is just as important as choosing the right types of plants for a butterfly flower garden. It is important you make note of where you are going to plant each flower and bush, especially when it comes to perennial varieties. You will need to have a basic map of where the perennials are planted so you do not mistakenly dig them up when preparing the soil for next year's butterfly garden.

Whether you are starting from seed or seedling, you will need to make sure you give your plants plenty of room to grow. Some varieties of butterfly flowers and plants tend to spread out as they grow while some remain more compact. Each plant will need to be researched to ensure the proper space is given in the butterfly garden.

The Butterfly Bush can grow as high as ten feet so it is important to keep the different needs of your plants in mind as you are setting up your garden. When in doubt, landscape design companies offer their services in planning and planting flowering gardens. This is ideal for those who do not feel confident doing these tasks themselves.

CHAPTER EIGHT
Tips for Maintaining a Butterfly Garden

Maintaining a butterfly garden is important for providing plant life for butterflies. With the right plants, the right space, and a little work, you will be able to enjoy butterflies as they flitter about your garden and provide you with their delightful colors and designs. Maintaining your garden will keep it looking beautiful through spring, summer, and fall.

~How to keep weeds out of your butterfly garden~

Pesticides are a big no-no when it comes to creating a butterfly garden. If you use pesticides to remove weeds, you will find butterflies stay away or begin to die. One of the most effective ways to keep weeds at bay is to use mulch. Mulch is a natural weed deterrent and offers an added benefit of keeping moisture in the soil. Covering your flower beds with a thick layer of organic mulch will help to keep weeds under control so you spend less time removing them and more time enjoying the beautiful butterflies the garden attracts.

Although there are non-chemical weed removers on the market, some of these contain ingredients that can actually repel butterflies and can even be dangerous to their health. Using rich organic mulch is by far the best method of controlling weeds while preventing any disruption to the health of butterflies in all cycles of life.

~Tips for safely feeding the plants in your butterfly garden~

Because the plants in your garden will become a food source and shelter for butterflies, it is important they are healthy and strong. Thankfully, there are organic means of feeding your plants and these methods will not cause any damage to the caterpillar larvae or adult butterflies.

Compost – Compost is one of the most effective means of nurturing the plant life in your butterfly garden. The plants butterflies love tend to favor soil that drains well and is full of organic material. Composting is also great for the environment and reduces waste put into landfills. For the best soil results, put about three inches of compost on top of the garden soil and mix it in well with the top six to eight inches of soil in the garden. Doing this will greatly enrich your soil and prepare it for giving nutrients to your plants.

Fertilizer – Because most of the plants you will be growing in your garden are of the flowering variety, it is vital the plants are properly fertilized. Although there are chemical fertilizers on the market, these sometimes contain ingredients that can be harmful to butterfly life. Ideally, using organic fertilizers is best. Phosphorous and Potassium are the two most important fertilizer components for nectar-producing flowers.

~Soil maintenance is important for healthy plants~

The soil in your garden is one of the most important aspects. If the soil is leached of nutrients, the plants in your garden will begin to die. These tips will help to ensure your garden soil is healthy and contains the nutrients it needs for growing beautiful butterfly plants.

Testing – Testing the pH level of the soil is vital for ensuring healthy plant life. The proper pH level of the soil should range from 6.5 to 6.8. When the pH level is out of this range, the minerals in the soil become bonded to the soil particles and are not able to be released to the plants. The kits for testing pH are fairly inexpensive and easy to use.

Professional soil testing – Having your garden soil professionally tested is a good idea because it can reveal a lot about the condition of your soil. This will allow you to know if you need to add fertilizer or other types of soil mixtures to your butterfly garden soil.

Soil testing tests for micronutrients such as manganese, zinc, and boron. To get the most accurate results, it is important to take soil samples from different areas of your butterfly garden. It is best to have a professional soil test carried out in spring and fall.

When taking care of the soil of your garden, it is important to realize you are not going to become an expert right away. If you have very little gardening experience, do not allow this to deter you. With the above tips and time, you can easily learn all the skills you need to keep your garden soil healthy for your plants.

Conclusion
A Butterfly Garden
Brings Joy for Years to Come

Witnessing the stages of a butterfly right before your eyes is one of the joys of butterfly gardening. If you love watching these special insects fly around, why not try to plant your own garden? Although it takes a little time and planning, having a butterfly garden in place will offer you many hours of joy over the years.

Butterfly gardens offer excellent learning opportunities for adults and children. Nothing could be more relaxing than sitting and enjoying a bright sunny morning filled with butterflies as they flitter about your garden, looking for sweet nectar.

As your garden grows, you will discover new elements to add to its beauty whether it be ornamental garden statues or beautiful pottery. Have fun and work to ensure your butterfly garden is a source of relaxation from a world that can sometimes feel a bit cold and overly chaotic.

Butterfly gardening allows us to realize the importance of slowing down from time to time so we can relish in the beauty God has provided us with. The butterfly embodies the beauty of this Earth and if we will just stop a moment and listen and watch, we can enjoy it for ourselves.

Thank you for buying this book. If you would take a minute to write a review, I would very much appreciate it. It really helps me with sales and promotion.

Respectfully,
Butch Spillman

About the Author
Butch Spillman

Butch Spillman is an author with a heart for people. Born in Hollywood, California in 1946, Butch always seemed to have a dream that kept him going, even when leaving home at the tender age of 14, because he had no other choice. Life wasn't easy but Butch refused to ever give up, no matter how tough the road became.

Butch's vast career first involved him becoming a radio DJ, working the graveyard shift to pay the bills and enjoy the life experience it brought him. He would go on to work in many cities, lighting up the airways with his intoxicating personality, filled with humor and understanding.

At the age of eighteen, Butch Spillman set out on a journey to work in real estate and even acquired a General Contractor's license so he could begin building houses. He enjoyed the challenge the real estate industry brought to his life and he experienced great success in his endeavors.

Throughout his career, Butch has never stopped learning. Life taught him from an early age that he had to do for himself and keep working diligently to be successful and that is just what he did. No challenge was too great and he never accepted failures, constantly striving to better himself in all he chose to pursue.

Today, Butch is retired and although he has slowed down, he certainly has not stopped. Married to a beautiful wife, he has two grown sons and four grandchildren he loves immensely. Throughout his life, Butch has always felt God's leading hand, guiding him on each path he has sought.

In the latest adventure of his life, Butch has set out to fulfill his lifelong dream of becoming a published author. With his skills and life knowledge, he seeks to educate, enlighten, entertain, and encourage readers of all ages.

Other Kindle eBooks and Paperbacks
by Butch Spillman

52 Bedtime Stories
Children's Read-Aloud Short Stories,
each with a Moral Christian Lesson

Jesus Christ, Always and Forever
How to Apply Biblical Truths
to Our Lives Today

67 Quick & Easy Italian Meals
Great Italian Recipes and Menu Ideas

1100 Fish Recipes

130 Salmon Recipes, 67 Cod Recipes, 50 Trout Recipes,
80 Halibut Recipes, 13 Red Snapper Recipes plus over 650 more Recipes for
33 other Fish types. Bonus Recipes include 100 Sauce Recipes,
14 Court Bouillon (Poaching Broth) Recipes,
100 Miscellaneous Fish Recipes and
27 Ways to Cook Frog Legs.

Dogs have Masters,
Cats have Staff

A Great Cat Training Guide dealing with
Cat Spraying, Cat Beds, Cat Litter, Clicker Training,
Cat Scratching and more...

"LOL"

Comedy can be Learned.

This Guide teaches why people laugh,

how to do stand-up, write jokes and routines,

handle hecklers, market yourself, and more.